P9-DFR-636

BLACK BEARS

LIVING WILD

Published by Creative Education and Creative Paperbacks
P.O. Box 227, Mankato, Minnesota 56002
Creative Education and Creative Paperbacks are imprints of The Creative Company
www.thecreativecompany.us

Design and production by Mary Herrmann
Art direction by Rita Marshall
Printed in China

Photographs by Alamy (ClassicStock, Design Pics Inc), Creative Commons Wikimedia (94th Airlift Wing/DVIDS, Appalachian Encounters/Flickr, Gillfoto, Maximilian Helm/Flickr, Guy M. Ingram/Oregon Sportsman, Jackmont, National Park Service), Dreamstime (Cvandyke, Steve Mann, Brandon Smith), Florida Fish & Wildlife Conservation Commission, Mary Herrmann, iStockphoto (BirdImages, bjmc, excentric_01, GeorgePeters, Lynn_Bystrom, mphillips007, MrsOKeefe, sassy1902), Off the Beaten Path Tours (Explore Haida Gwaii), Shutterstock (Karel Bartik, J. Bicking, Mircea Costina, critterbiz, Jim Cumming, Chase Dekker, Dennis W Donohue, emperorcosar, forestpath, Lois GoBe, I WALL, Kane513, Cynthia Kidwell, Geoffrey Kuchera, Miosotis_Jade, nialat, paulista, Menno Schaefer, Tigger11th, weter777, Wild Art), U.S. National Park Service (Theodore Roosevelt Birthplace)

Library of Congress Cataloging-in-Publication Data
Names: Gish, Melissa, author.
Title: Black bears / Melissa Gish.
Series: Living wild.
Includes bibliographical references and index.
Summary: A look at black bears, including their habitats, physical characteristics such as their muzzles and paws, behaviors, relationships with humans, and the recent threat of Asian folk medicine trade on these curious bears today.
Identifiers: LCCN 2017035407 / ISBN 978-1-60818-956-4 (hardcover) / ISBN 978-1-62832-561-4 (pbk) / ISBN 978-1-64000-035-3 (eBook)

Subjects: LCSH: Black bear—Juvenile literature.
Classification: LCC QL737.C27 G52 2018 / DDC 599.78/5—dc23

CCSS: RI.5.1, 2, 3, 8; RST.6-8.1, 2, 5, 6, 8; RH.6-8.3, 4, 5, 6, 7, 8

First Edition HC 9 8 7 6 5 4 3 2 1
First Edition PBK 9 8 7 6 5 4 3 2 1

CREATIVE EDUCATION • CREATIVE PAPERBACKS

BLACK BEARS

Melissa Gish

It is a cool October morning in Ocala
National Forest. A Florida black bear

slaps its paw into a school of golden shiners

in the warm water of Juniper Springs.

It is a cool October morning in Ocala National Forest. A Florida black bear slaps its paw into a school of golden shiners in the warm water of Juniper Springs. The fish scatter, their reflective scales shimmering like bits of glass in the dawn light. The bear lowers its head and begins to drink. Soon, hunger sets in; it is time for breakfast. At nearly 300 pounds (136 kg), the bear could easily devour just about anything it comes across. What it really wants, though, are about the size of marbles: saw palmetto berries. Turning away from the water's edge, the bear follows its nose through the lush vegetation. Most of the saw palmettos have been picked clean, but the bear gets lucky. It finds a hidden trove of berries. Each berry has a hard, oil-rich seed inside. The bear begins chomping, filling its stomach with the crunchy berries.

WHERE IN THE WORLD THEY LIVE

■ **Queen Charlotte Black Bear**
Haida Gwaii (Queen Charlotte Islands)

Glacier Bear
southeastern Alaska

■ **Cinnamon Bear**
southwestern Canada and northwestern United States

■ **Kermode Bear**
British Columbia

■ **Florida Black Bear**
Florida, southern Georgia, and southern Alabama

The 16 American black bear subspecies range throughout North American woodlands from Canada to Mexico, with the largest populations in Alaska and British Columbia. Some subspecies are more widespread than others, but almost all of these clever, curious bears have continued to thrive alongside humans. The colored squares represent the typical locations of five black bear subspecies living in the wild today.

CINNAMON AND HONEY

Brown bears had existed in North America for about 2.5 million years by the time the American black bear **evolved** roughly 500,000 years ago. Black bears once roamed the entire continent, but today, most are found in forested areas of Alaska and Canada, with only scattered populations throughout the continental United States and northern Mexico. The earliest bear ancestor, *Ursavus elmensis*, or the dawn bear, lived in Asia about 23 to 5.3 million years ago. The size of a house cat, this animal was the forerunner of the many bear species that spread around the globe.

Bears belong to the genus *Ursus*, which is Latin for "bear." The eight species of modern bear are the sun bear of Southeast Asia; the spectacled bear of South America; the sloth bear of India; the polar bear of the Arctic regions; the panda of China; the Asiatic black bear of northeastern Russia to Malaysia; the brown bear, found throughout North America, Europe, and Asia; and the American black bear, of which there are 16 subspecies.

The American black bear subspecies are classified not only by geography but also by differences in the

A black bear relative, the rare spectacled bear is the only bear species native to South America.

Most glacier bears reside in Glacier Bay National Park and Tongass National Forest.

Because bears eat a variety of fruits and plants, they improve the health of their forest habitats by dispersing seeds in their feces.

bears' **genetic** makeup. Isolated from other bears, each subspecies developed distinct features based on its environment and diet. For example, fish-eating Queen Charlotte black bears of the island group Haida Gwaii in British Columbia have larger teeth than other black bears. Glacier bears, which inhabit southeastern coastal Alaska, have a gray-blue tint to their fur, perhaps to better blend in with their frozen habitat. Occupying evergreen forests from Wyoming to British Columbia, cinnamon bears have brownish coats. Most black bears are black, though some individuals have a white mark on their chest. Uniquely, a number of Kermode bears, found on various islands off the coast of British Columbia, have white coats. They are called spirit bears.

The American black bear's closest relative is the Asiatic black bear. These bears are black with a white V-shaped marking on their chests. Scientists believe that Asiatic black bears were the first of the modern bears to evolve. There are only about 50,000 remaining on the planet. American black bears are more abundant. Roughly 870,000 black bears exist in North America, with about half of them in the U.S. However, the small populations

Asiatic black bears are nicknamed "moon bears" for the pale, crescent-shaped marking on their chests.

Even black bears within the same family group can have variations in fur color.

of three subspecies—the New Mexico, Florida, and Louisiana black bears—are protected from hunting in their home states. In Mexico, black bears are listed as an endangered species.

Because black bears can be brown and brown bears are sometimes black, the two species are sometimes mistaken for one another. What sets these bears apart is the brown bear's distinctive shoulder hump. Black bears lack this hump. Brown bears also have a slightly concave forehead, whereas black bears' foreheads are straight. Powerful shoulder and jaw muscles are useful to brown bears, which typically hunt large animals such as elk and deer. Black bears, with their smaller **muzzle**, typically eat much smaller prey.

Black bears are omnivores, which means they eat both animals and plants. About 80 to 85 percent of these opportunistic eaters' diets consist of plants, berries, and nuts. They also scavenge dead animals, hunt small mammals such as ground squirrels and marmots, and capture fish from rivers and streams. In spring, they may prey on young deer and caribou and, as many stories depict, raid beehives for honey.

Only about 1 in 10 Kermode bears is born with white or cream-colored fur.

The Kitasoo, a First Nations people of British Columbia, call the white Kermode bear *moksgm'ol*, which means spirit, or ghost, bear.

Young bears lose their primary teeth and grow permanent teeth by age three.

The black bear has 42 teeth that allow it to eat almost anything. Two pairs of long, sharp canine teeth and six pairs of pointed incisors are used for tearing meat. Along the sides of the jaw, eight pairs of small, flat teeth and five pairs of large molars crush and grind vegetation and nuts. Flexible lips and a long, agile tongue capture hard-to-reach **larvae** and other small food items.

Bears are mammals, or animals that, with the exceptions of the egg-laying platypus and echidna, give birth to live young and produce milk to feed them. Like all mammals, bears are warm-blooded. This means that their bodies maintain a constant temperature that is usually warmer than their surroundings. Like most of their relatives, black bears develop a thick layer of fat just beneath the skin. This fat protects against heat loss and provides **nutrients** through the winter, when they enter an inactive state called torpor.

American black bears are about five feet (1.5 m) long and typically stand three to four feet (0.9–1.2 m) tall at the shoulder. Male bears, which are called boars, are heavier than females, called sows. In summer, when food is plentiful, males typically weigh up to 500 pounds

Climate change is contributing to an increase in ticks and mites, which black bears scratch off by any means possible.

Without claws, the skeletal structure of a black bear's paw looks similar to that of a human hand.

During torpor, black bears shed the thick skin covering the pads of their feet and grow new pad coverings.

(227 kg), and females can weigh up to 250 pounds (113 kg). Black bears that regularly eat human food (usually by raiding garbage or being fed by people) have been recorded at more than 800 pounds (363 kg). By comparison, the world's largest bear, the polar bear, can weigh up to 1,700 pounds (771 kg).

Black bears walk on the soles of the feet, a mammalian characteristic called plantigrade. This allows them to distribute their weight over a wide area and run swiftly—up to 35 miles (56.3 km) per hour—despite being so bulky. Each paw is at least five inches (12.7 cm) wide and has five digits. The digit ends in a sharp claw about one and a quarter inches (3.2 cm) long. Black bears are also strong swimmers, and, although most bears climb trees when they are young, black bears are the only bears that continue to climb trees as adults.

Black bears are highly inquisitive. They have good eyesight, and their sense of smell is well developed. When bears stand up on their hind legs, it is usually to smell scents carried by the wind. The black bear's sense of smell is 21 times more sensitive than a human's. It can detect garbage buried under nearly a foot (30.5 cm) of

soil. Furthermore, a bear's **olfactory system** is connected to the part of the brain that stores memories. This means that in addition to finding new food sources, bears can remember where the best berries or nuts can be found from year to year. Bears that are relocated often return to familiar places by using their memory and sense of smell. Scientists also believe that when bears smell changes in weather, they recognize the time for winter sleep.

Scientists have found that bears that routinely raid human trash are overweight and unhealthy.

Bears will eat every last bit of food they can find before beginning their long winter nap.

SLEEPING BEAUTIES

The black bear is a solitary animal, living alone in a particular area called a home range. The size of a black bear's home range depends on the amount of food resources available. Females' home ranges typically vary from 2.5 to 10 square miles (6.5–25.9 sq km). Males may claim up to 60 square miles (155 sq km). Ideal bear habitat has a combination of forest, meadow, and water such as a river or lake.

In late summer and early fall, bears consume three times more food per day than they do in spring and early summer. They spend up to 20 hours a day eating. This behavior, called hyperphagia, is how they prepare for winter. They will gain roughly a third of their normal body weight. Some bears even double their weight by winter. What triggers the winter sleep in November or December is not entirely understood. Scientists believe that changes in the amount of sunlight and its angle prompt chemical changes in bears' bodies. The length of torpor is related to the weather conditions each fall and spring. In the days leading up to torpor, bears stop eating and drink very little. They let their digestive systems

The fatter a female becomes throughout summer and fall, the more cubs she is capable of having in winter.

Females that are ready to breed dribble urine as they patrol the borders of their territory, which alerts males to their location.

Black bears tend to rest during the day and forage for food at twilight.

Scientists from University of Alaska Fairbanks found that bears in torpor can drop their heart rates from 55 beats per minute to just 9!

empty. Blood flow to their limbs decreases, and their **organs** begin to slow down.

Bears choose a den that is dry and somewhat confined. The less open space around the bear, the less heat the animal will lose. Contrary to popular belief, most black bears do not choose to spend winter in caves. They prefer brush piles and hollow logs from fallen trees. Where trees are quite large, bears may climb up to 60 feet (18.3 m) high and enter cavities in the trunks. Some bears dig dens under tree roots or drag brush into culverts or under rock ledges. Black bears have even been known to simply lie down in a depression in the earth and let snow cover them.

True hibernators such as ground squirrels and bats cannot be awakened from sleep—even if touched—until their bodies tell them that it is time to eat or defecate. Bears sometimes awaken if disturbed, but what makes them truly unique is that they can sleep for months without eating, drinking, urinating, or defecating. This is because their bodies are perfect recyclers. While sleeping for five to eight months, a bear's **metabolism** functions at half its normal rate. Its body burns only fat for energy. A result of burning fat is an increase in fluid, which the

Rocky shelters make excellent dens because they are well-insulated and provide protection from wind.

bear absorbs, so it does not need to drink water. The little urine that is produced is absorbed by bladder tissue and turned into water, carbon dioxide, and ammonia. The ammonia is in turn recycled to form amino acids, which are the building blocks of protein. This protein is used to repair muscle cells that are damaged from lack of use, and other chemicals protect bones from deteriorating. So when a bear awakens in spring, its body is still in perfect working order—it's just very hungry! Perhaps even more amazing than the black bear's period of torpor is what can happen during this time: females may give birth.

Bear cubs learn to climb trees early in life not only for protection but also to find food.

Black bears mate at four to six years of age. In June or July, boars seek out sows in and around their home ranges. Sows typically mate with more than one boar and may produce a number of offspring from different fathers. Once bears mate, they go their separate ways again. If the sow does not put on sufficient weight by winter, her body will resorb her fertilized eggs. But if she is fat enough when winter comes, she will have as many as six offspring. The cubs will be born while the sow is sleeping, sometime between late December and early February.

Cubs are born blind. Their bodies are covered in fine, gray fur. They are typically about eight inches (20.3 cm) long and weigh less than a can of soda. The mother will continue to sleep as the cubs are nourished by the protein-rich milk she produces. She will wake groggily to shift her weight to avoid crushing her cubs. She will clean them and eat their feces so that predators such as wolves and cougars do not smell the cubs and invade the den. Because mother bears cannot sleep as soundly as other bears, they may lose more than 30 percent of their body weight over winter. Other bears lose just 15 to 20 percent.

When black bear cubs first emerge from a den, they are typically no larger than a housecat.

Black bears grasp tree trunks with their curled front claws and then walk up the tree with their back paws—like inchworms.

Black bears may remain active into December if conditions are mild and food remains accessible; they may sleep longer if spring warming comes late.

Bear cubs grow quickly. When they emerge from the den with their mother in early spring, they are about 2 months old and weigh up to 10 pounds (4.5 kg). The mother defends the cubs from threats, especially male black bears, which kill more cubs than any other predator. Cubs typically react to danger by climbing trees, but sometimes they simply bawl until their mother comes to rescue them. Mothers have been known to gently hold cubs in their mouths to help them descend from trees or relocate. Cubs follow their mother, learning which foods are good to eat and where to find the best food sources. They continue to nurse, but they also eat solid food to fatten up in preparation for winter.

At almost a year old, the cubs are still about 10 times smaller than their mother. She prepares a den in the fall, and she and her cubs all enter torpor together. Even without a mother, an orphaned cub knows how to make a den. But unless the solitary cub weighs about 30 pounds (13.6 kg), its survival through the winter is unlikely. Smaller cubs need their mother to keep them warm in the den. By the next spring, the mother is ready to mate again, so she chases her offspring away. They are now 17

Black bears are most at risk from predators during the first three years of their lives.

to 18 months old and must care for themselves. The next few years will be the most dangerous time of their lives.

Some scientists think bears remember their family members throughout their lives. Females establish home ranges near their mothers. Some even overlap their mother's home range with little conflict. Males may travel as far as 150 miles (241 km) to claim their own territories. Adult black bears have two major predators: brown bears and humans. The average life span of wild black bears is 18 years, but those living far from humans have been known to live into their 30s.

Ursa Major, of which the Big Dipper is a part, is visible at night in most of the Northern Hemisphere.

Since humans first arrived in North America, the black bear has been part of people's spirituality and **mythology**. Bears were respected not only for their physical strength but also for their spiritual power. Many American Indian **cultures** believed that bears controlled the sunlight. In winter, when the bear slept, the days were short, and in spring, when the bear awakened, the days grew longer. A story from the Menominee people tells that when the Great Spirit created the black bear, the creature took the name Sekatcokemau. This "brother bear" built the first wigwam to shelter his people and created the canoe so that people could catch fish.

A legend from the Meskwaki people, who originated in southeastern Ontario, tells how the constellation of stars known as Ursa Major, or the Great Bear, came to be. Three brothers went bear hunting in winter. One brother went into a bear's den and chased it out. The bear ran north, and the brothers followed it. Then the bear ran east, and the brothers continued their pursuit. When the bear ran west, the brothers stayed close behind. Soon

Haida artist Bill Reid's Bear *(1963) is displayed at the University of British Columbia's Museum of Anthropology.*

A photograph of a mounted lava bear appeared in a 1917 issue of The Oregon Sportsman *magazine.*

Hawks and eagles can carry off bear cubs, and in the southern U.S., alligators have been known to attack small black bears.

the brothers realized they had run high into the sky and could not get back to Earth. To this day, they continue to chase the bear around the North Star.

A modern legend arose in the early 20th century. In 1917, people began seeing miniature bears in southern Oregon. Because the bears were spotted around lava beds formed from ancient volcanic activity, they were called lava bears. Over the next 17 years, many were shot or trapped. Their fur was scruffy and pale. They stood about 18 inches (45.7 cm) tall and weighed only about 25 pounds (11.3 kg). News of these strange animals appeared in the *Oregon Sportsman* and *Saturday Evening Post* magazines. The Smithsonian Institution even offered a reward for a live lava bear. Alas, in 1934, after scientific examination of several specimens, it was determined that the so-called lava bears were actually black bear cubs and yearlings suffering from malnutrition because of the poor quality of the lava bed habitat.

When European settlers spread across what would become the eastern U.S., they did not realize that black bears are not as aggressive and dangerous as the European brown bears with which they were familiar. The settlers

shot all bears on sight. Black bears learned to avoid humans and their guns, retreating into the dense forests. By the mid-1800s, black bears had become more of a pest than a threat, and people began viewing them as dim-witted, lumbering oafs. In the 1860s and '70s, American artist William Holbrook Beard's fanciful paintings of bears performing human activities became popular. In Beard's world, bears danced, played games, went to school, had picnics, played musical instruments, and even

Studies have shown that black bears typically select natural food sources but sometimes seek treats around human dwellings.

"THE LITTLE BEAR WONDER OF OREGON"

No one has yet named him, so we will call him "Teddy" for the present, believing that in the near future naturalists will probably find a more appropriate name, and, it is presumed, will be able to tell us something of his kind.

Teddy was a real bear, full grown, little larger than a badger, only weighing 23 pounds when killed.

The home of this species of bear is in the lava beds near Fossil Lake, well out on the Oregon desert....

Teddy is not the only bear of his kind killed on the desert, but several others have been taken, all of which were taken by inexperienced people and thought to be cubs....

This sort of bear may be of a distinct specie, and he may not. I am not now in possession of any authentic natural history, but ... my theory is that the lineage of this bear will be traced back to the common black or brown bear of the Cascades. Possibly ... generation after generation the race has been feebly perpetuated, largely through inbreeding in this dry, waste country, with no water and meagre forage, until they have dwarfed to their present size, and would ultimately become extinct.

Teddy was killed this year, sometime in May, ... at the time presumed to be a cub. However, after a careful search for the mother and an examination of the supposed cub, he was found to be an old bear....

This little bear looks just like any other bear, with the exception of his size and color. His hair has the appearance of wool more than hair, and its color is of a light buckskin cast. He is gray around the nose and his teeth and claws are worn.

It is believed that the state should make an effort to secure some live specimens of these bears, for without a doubt others interested will immediately begin trying to secure these rare specimens.

from The Oregon Sportsman *(January 1917), by Guy M. Ingram* got the best of a bear hunter by carrying him off toward the woods. His painting titled "So You Wanna Get Married, Eh?" depicts a young bear couple asking their elder for permission to marry.

The public's view of bears continued to soften in the 20th century. In November 1902, president Theodore Roosevelt went bear hunting in Mississippi with the state's governor. After three days, Roosevelt still had not spotted a bear. He was quite unhappy, so without his knowing, Roosevelt's hosts tracked down a black bear and tied it to a tree. Then they led Roosevelt to the bear. But the bear was old, thin, and terrified. Roosevelt refused to shoot it because he felt that to do so would be unsportsmanlike. Despite the fact that he ordered someone else to shoot it, Roosevelt was hailed as a hero. When toymaker Morris Michtom heard the story, he got Roosevelt's permission to use the president's name, and the Teddy bear was born. A few years later, in 1907, composer John Walter Bratton wrote "The Teddy Bears' Picnic." Lyrics were added to the song by Jimmy Kennedy in 1932.

The black bear also inspired one of the world's best-known bear characters: Winnie-the-Pooh. Writer A. A.

A cartoon of Roosevelt refusing to shoot a tethered bear first appeared in the Washington Post *on November 16, 1902.*

In 2010, the United Kingdom honored Winnie-the-Pooh with a series of 10 postage stamps.

The American black bear became the official state animal of New Mexico in 1963 and of West Virginia in 1973.

Milne based his famous character on a black bear named Winnipeg. The bear was captured in Ontario in 1914 and donated to the London Zoo, where Milne took his son Christopher to see the bear. While Winnie-the-Pooh looks nothing like a real black bear, the two share a similar curiosity and exceptionally gentle nature.

In 1944, Smokey Bear was created by the U.S. Forest Service as part of a campaign to educate people about the dangers of forest fires. Sporting a park ranger's hat, Smokey soon became a recognized figure, but his popularity soared six years later when people met a real-life Smokey Bear. In 1950, a fire was raging in New Mexico's Lincoln National Forest. A group of soldiers from Fort Bliss, Texas, was helping fight the fire when they spotted a bear cub trapped up a tree. The cub's paws and legs were burned, so when the soldiers rescued him, they named him Hotfoot Teddy. Park rangers cared for the cub, and when news of the rescue was publicized, the National Zoo in Washington, D.C., offered to adopt the bear. He was renamed Smokey after the U.S. Forest Service mascot. He lived at the zoo for 26 years, where he received so much fan mail that the postal service assigned Smokey his own zip code.

Another real-life black bear that received fan mail he couldn't read was Bruno the bear. The 1965 novel *Gentle Ben* by Walt Morey features a brown bear named Ben. When the book became the movie *Gentle Giant* in 1967, Ben went from brown bear to black bear, and Bruno was the star. Bruno went on to portray Ben in the television series *Gentle Ben* from 1967 to 1969. When the show ended, Bruno continued to appear in movies and television shows for 10 more years. Today, the American black bear is still considered the "gentle" one when compared with its polar- and brown-bear cousins.

Born in Wisconsin in 1962, Bruno lost his mother and was raised by a game farmer before being sold to a Hollywood animal trainer.

Today, a typical bearskin cap stands about 18 inches (45.7 cm) tall and weighs roughly 1.5 pounds (0.7 kg).

Unlike many of North America's other large mammals, black bears have managed to remain relatively abundant since Europeans first arrived in the New World. From the 16th through the 18th centuries, the fur trade put thousands of Europeans to work trapping and hunting fur-bearing animals in Canada and the U.S. While black bears were not in demand as much as animals such as beavers and otters, they did have one major use: bearskin caps. Beginning in the mid-1700s, the armies of Britain, Denmark, Spain, Italy, Belgium, and other countries began wearing tall hats made of black bear fur. As the practice continued, American black bear numbers dropped. By the 1960s, Canada and the U.S. each had only about 150,000 black bears. Limits were placed on bear hunting, and black bear populations have bounced back, now numbering nearly one million.

A fairly new and much more deadly threat has cast its shadow over the American black bear: the Asian folk medicine trade. The demand for bear body parts has led to plummeting populations of Asiatic black bears, and now brown and black bears in North America are

The art of preserving animal skins in their original lifelike shape is called taxidermy.

Park rangers estimate that 10 percent of black bears in Yosemite National Park risk automobile collisions each year.

Black bears have been known to break car windows, climb inside, and pull out the back seats to get to food stored in the trunk.

being **poached**. The most desired part of a bear is its gall bladder. This organ produces bile, a liquid that aids in the digestion of food. Bears have been killed for their gall bladders for thousands of years, with the belief that black bears produce the most potent bile. With wild populations nearly extinguished, China now runs bear farms, where tubes are inserted into caged bears to drain their bile. Animal-rights organizations have protested this **unethical** practice, yet the industry continues to grow. The Trade Records Analysis of Flora and Fauna in Commerce (TRAFFIC) reported that one gram (0.04 oz)—about the size of one M&M's® candy piece—of bear bile could sell in Asia for more than $150 U.S. That's four times the price of pure gold! Conservationists are concerned that bears in North America could eventually suffer the same population decline as their Asian cousins, if the international trade in bear parts is not stopped.

American black bears are game animals, and tens of thousands are taken by licensed hunters annually in the U.S. and Canada. State wildlife officials establish an appropriate number each year to make sure bears do not overpopulate and suffer from a lack of resources. In

the wild, black bears may enter campsites looking for food, but usually campers can chase them away. Wildlife specialists advise people to never run, because the bear may instinctively give chase. Instead, keeping eyes on the bear and slowly backing away is the best option. Black bears will typically run the other direction to get away from people. Only about 70 people have been killed by black bears since 1900. Most cases involved young male bears that had likely never seen humans before and simply viewed the person as a prey animal. Black bears are the only bear species known

With a sense of smell seven times stronger than a dog's, bears can detect even the smallest bit of food in a campsite.

Curious bears living near humans quickly learn to dismantle bird feeders and push open sliding doors.

to feed on humans—other bears may kill in self-defense but typically leave the body untouched.

As humans continue to **encroach** on bear habitat, black bears may become less fearful of people. They are drawn to anything that smells like food, including trash, pet food, bird feeders, and outdoor grills. Black bears are not put off by puzzles, either. They will work to open containers if they know a delicious prize awaits them. And they may even choose the better of two options, based on the amount of the reward. In 2012, **psychologists** Jennifer Vonk of Oakland University and Michael J. Beran of Georgia State

University studied black bears to determine if they could understand counting. They trained black bears to touch computer screens with their noses. Then they presented two options to the bears: one screen with a few large images and another screen with many smaller images. Overwhelmingly, the bears chose the screen with the many smaller images, representing many tidbits rather than a few. This suggests that bears understand that count has a relationship to quantity and that bigger does not necessarily mean more—and black bears always want more.

An ongoing study of black bears by the Minnesota Department of Natural Resources (DNR) followed the life of the world's longest-lived bear. Known as Bear 56, the female black bear born in 1974 lived 39.5 years—longer than any other wild bear of any species in the world. Since the research program in northern Minnesota began in 1981, about 360 black bears have been captured, measured, blood-tested, and fitted with numbered ear tags and tracking collars. Information from the study and others like it assists wildlife officials in determining the density, health, and genetic makeup of black bear populations. Bear 56 was among the first subjects when the study began. Over the

An interactive online map allows people to track collared black bears in Yosemite National Park.

Black bears raid birds' nests, ant colonies, and the wispy nests of tent caterpillars, consuming as many as 25,000 insects per day.

A black bear's ears can be a quick indicator of age: the larger the ears in relation to the head, the younger the bear.

course of her life, she produced 23 cubs and outlived them all. DNR officer Karen Noyce, who located Bear 56 after she had passed away, explained that Bear 56 lived so long because she was shy, stayed away from humans, and did not eat bait from hunters' traps. In addition, the DNR had asked local hunters to not shoot her. The only bear in the study to pass away from old age, Bear 56 died peacefully in her sleep. Her story can be found on the Minnesota DNR's website.

Bears' amazing ability to survive lengthy periods of torpor has long fascinated scientists. Now researchers are focusing on the chemical processes that protect black bears' bones during their winter sleep. An understanding of how to reproduce these processes in humans could allow astronauts to spend more time in space without the risk of their bones becoming brittle. SpaceWorks Enterprises, an American engineering company that develops projects for space travel, wants to reach even farther. The company is studying ways to induce a bear-like torpor in humans. By lowering metabolism and slowing body systems—just like bears do—humans could travel great distances through space with very few resources and little impact on their bodies and minds. This research is in its very early stages,

To protect themselves from non-tree-climbing brown bears, black bears may sleep in trees.

but SpaceWorks president John Bradford says the program is "very promising."

For thousands of years, people's views of black bears have ranged from fear to annoyance to fascination as we have discovered black bears' unique role in the forest **ecosystem**. We still have much to learn about these remarkable animals and how their biological secrets may benefit us. But more importantly, we can discover how to help them continue to thrive in an ever-changing world.

ANIMAL TALE: THE BOY WHO LIVED WITH THE BEARS

The Passamaquoddy are an American Indian people from the coastal region of Maine and New Brunswick. Relying mostly on fish as a source of meat, they sometimes also hunted black bears. Passed down from their oral tradition, this story tells of the relationship between humans and black bears and why custom forbids bear hunters to kill females or their cubs.

One spring day, a little boy wandered away from his family as they fished along the riverbank. He soon found himself lost in the forest. Just as the last rays of sunlight disappeared from the sky, the boy came upon a cave. He peeked his head inside, hoping to find shelter from the cold. Suddenly, a black bear emerged. The boy was terrified, but the bear made no move to attack him. Instead, it waved its paw, inviting the boy inside its den. The bear was a female with two cubs. To protect the boy from the cold, she nudged him toward her cubs. The boy snuggled up and felt very warm. Soon he fell asleep.

The boy stayed with the bears. All summer, while the bears fattened themselves on berries, the boy gathered food for himself. He collected berries, acorns, nuts, and fish, which he dried and smoked in a fire pit. He knew that when winter came, the bears would sleep without eating. But he could not. He would need food all winter. The bears also knew this, so they helped him gather food and store it in the den.

Some years passed, and the boy grew big and strong, like his adoptive bear mother. He even began to grow hair on his body like the bears. And he all but forgot what it was like to be human. Then one day, he heard voices in the forest. Suddenly, he remembered his first family. The voices got closer, and the boy turned to the she-bear with a smile on his face. But she was not smiling. She was afraid. Men appeared with bows and arrows, and they were pointing their weapons at her.

The boy leaped in front of the she-bear, shielding her. At first, the men were confused, but then they recognized the boy and lowered their bows. They rushed to embrace their lost brother. He told them how the she-bear had saved him and protected him all this time. He said goodbye to his bear family and went home with his people. The people were amazed at the boy's growth and strength. They said, "If he had stayed with the bears one more year, he would have turned into a bear!"

The boy was happy to be home with his human family, but he also missed his bear family. His brothers told him about their adventures every spring hunting black bears. This made the boy concerned about the she-bear. He vowed that he would never eat bear meat, and he made his brothers promise to never kill a she-bear, for it might be his bear-mother. He did not want to see her harmed. Today, the Passamaquoddy allow people with permits to hunt bears on their Maine tribal land in the spring, but females with cubs remain off limits.

GLOSSARY

cultures – particular groups in a society that share behaviors and characteristics that are accepted as normal by those groups

ecosystem – a community of organisms that live together in an environment

encroach – to move into an area already occupied

evolved – gradually developed into a new form

feces – waste matter eliminated from the body

genetic – relating to genes, the basic physical units of heredity

larvae – the newly hatched, wingless, often wormlike form of many insects before they become adults

metabolism – the processes that keep a body alive, including making use of food for energy

muzzle – the projecting part of an animal's face that includes the nose and mouth

mythology – a collection of myths, or popular, traditional beliefs or stories that explain how something came to be or that are associated with a person or object

nutrients – substances that give a living thing energy and help it grow

olfactory system – the body's system of cells, nerves, and organs related to the sense of smell

organs – parts of a living being that exist to perform specific tasks in the living being's body

poached – hunted protected species of wild animals, even though doing so was against the law

psychologists – people who study the mind and its functions, especially those affecting behavior

unethical – not agreeing with or not performing the actions and behaviors that are generally accepted by society

SELECTED BIBLIOGRAPHY

"American Black Bear." National Geographic. http://www.nationalgeographic.com/animals/mammals/a/american-black-bear/.

Beider, Robert E. *Bear.* London: Reaktion Books, 2005.

"Black Bear – *Ursus americanus*." Western Wildlife Outreach. http://westernwildlife.org/black-bear-outreach-project/black-bear-ursus-americanus/.

Garshelis, Dave. "The Shy Bear." *Minnesota Conservation Volunteer,* November–December 2015. Minnesota Department of Natural Resources. http://www.dnr.state.mn.us/mcvmagazine/issues/2015/nov-dec/black-bear-research.html.

Goodness, Tracie. "*Ursus thibetanus* – Asiatic black bear." Animal Diversity Web. http://animaldiversity.org/accounts/Ursus_thibetanus/.

Taylor, Dave. *Black Bears: A Natural History.* Brighton, Mass.: Fitzhenry & Whiteside, 2006.

Note: Every effort has been made to ensure that any websites listed above were active at the time of publication. However, because of the nature of the Internet, it is impossible to guarantee that these sites will remain active indefinitely or that their contents will not be altered.

From birth through adulthood, black bears contribute to the health of their forest ecosystem.

INDEX